"WHERE DID MY DAY GO?"

The Essentials of Leadership

21st Century Time Management

MARK J HOLLINGSWORTH

ISBN: 1490472959
ISBN-13: 978-1490472959

DEDICATION

To my wife Sue for her wonderful support.

CONTENTS

ACKNOWLEDGMENTS

I would like to thank CreateSpace and Amazon who have made it possible for new authors to realize their dreams of being published.

MARK HOLLINGSWORTH

INTRODUCTION

Welcome to my series of essential leadership skills' books, and to this book on the subject of 21st century time management. The aims and objectives of these books are to provide, through the format of story telling, a guide to acquiring the essential skills needed to be effective in leadership.

These books are based around a character called Quinn Spencer. Quinn has recently been appointed as the divisional manager of 'Geographical Area A' for a company called the Stratum Group Inc. (a fictitious organization). Stratum provides a variety of training solutions across a number of industries. They develop custom-made solutions as well as providing off-the-shelf versions. There are four geographical areas in Stratum, all controlled by the vice-president of sales and marketing Andrew Sachs. Quinn reports directly to Andrew.

Within this book, the second in the series, you will see Quinn, after the first month in the role of Divisional Manager, struggling with the volume of work needed to both manage the day-to-day activities whilst simultaneously lead the team in their many projects and tasks. Quinn discovers time management is as much about self-management as it is about project-management. In addition, without the ability to be able to bring singular focus to the most important tasks and objectives, life can quickly spiral out of control into a cluttered and disorganized mess!

With the help of the vice-president and a fellow divisional manager Quinn attempts to find that all-important focus through a combination of technology, processes and systems and the development of effective habits.

At the end of this book I have summarized the key learning points in an easy-to-use reference style.

Now let's join Quinn at the beginning of another working week at Stratum Group Inc.

Mark J Hollingsworth

The MJH Leadership Training Centre

Author's Note:

In this book I have referred to various technology products. I selected these products after extensive testing and found them to best meet the needs of the situation Quinn faced. The use of such products remains my personal choice – I am not necessarily endorsing them.

PART ONE
A CHAOTIC EXISTENCE

1. MONDAY MORNING

It was 7:15 AM on Monday morning and Quinn was desperate for the first cup of coffee of the day. 15 minutes ago, just before taking a shower, Quinn had turned the coffee filter machine on, and was now pulling together an appropriate outfit for the day.

Quinn's clothes were carelessly strewn across the closet, there were also some on the floor and some hanging out of the laundry basket – overall the bedroom was in a general state of confusion. Quinn decided that dark grey was the best colour for the day, and some fifteen minutes later eventually managed to pull together enough pieces from the chaos to emerge suitably dressed. Now, rushing because of the lost time spent pulling together the outfit, Quinn burst into the kitchen area for coffee. Quinn placed two slices of bread into the electric toaster and turned expectantly to the coffee machine, mug in hand.

The coffee machine had performed its function correctly and the coffee pot on the hotplate was full of hot liquid. The problem was the liquid was clear water! Damn, thought Quinn, realizing that having put in the filter cone Quinn had forgotten to put in the coffee granules! At least the toast popped up nicely brown, thanks to the inbuilt timer in the electric toaster. Quinn sat down with a glass of milk, in place of the much-needed coffee, and the two slices of toast and opened the laptop, which sat on the kitchen table.

A black screen stared at Quinn and, despite overly aggressively hitting several keys on the keyboard, the laptop refused to come to life. Quinn's heart was now beginning to race. Without access to the laptop it was impossible to see the day's schedule. Quinn now regretted not checking the schedule the night before, or even having some form of backup, perhaps in the form of a traditional paper day-timer. The fact the smart phone belonging to Quinn had fallen out of Quinn's briefcase two days ago smashing the screen and was now being repaired added to the trauma of the morning. This is no way to start a working week, mused Quinn.

At 7:45 AM, clutching a armful of files, and bursting full briefcase, which included the broken laptop, Quinn left the house and began the thirty minute commute to work. Quinn's mind was all over the place. Quinn's position as divisional manager at Stratum Group was now in its second month and appeared to be going well. Quinn had begun to feel more comfortable in delegating tasks to various members of the team and this certainly helped both lessen the immediate workload and enable focus to be given to the more essential tasks in Quinn's role.

However, Quinn still felt that much of the activity of the division was frustratingly at an arm's length and obtaining timely and accurate data on the performance of the division's departments was patchy to say the least. Although the delegation was helping, Quinn still had a sense of entering each day with a plan, but that plan was pretty much shot to pieces by 10 AM! Quinn justified the volumes of work being taken home every evening as a 'settling in' issue and one that would not last many more weeks.

Moreover, Quinn always seemed to be in a rush. Today was no exception, and Quinn knew that allowing just forty-five minutes to wake up, shower, dress and eat breakfast was insufficient time. The problem was, Quinn felt, exhaustion set in most evenings - Quinn was checking and replying to e-mails as late as

1 AM – and despite good intentions to rise earlier each morning it was in fact getting harder and harder to awake at the normal time. Furthermore, extensive reading of background material, trade journals, management reports were taking place in the quietness of Quinn's house rather than at the more chaotic office.

Intense activity today began in Quinn's office upon arrival at 8:30 AM. Having started up the desktop computer Quinn firstly accessed the e-mail account and then listened/downloaded the unanswered voice mails from yesterday. Although nobody visited Quinn's office over the next hour and a half there were many virtual visitors in the form of chains of e-mails and the inevitable game of voicemail tag.

After nearly two months in the role Quinn's office still resembled a badly organized storage unit! Papers Quinn returned with from the night before were emptied out of the briefcase on to one flat surface area, files, many with no identifying labels, lay on the floor, or the desk, and any other available flat surface. A growing pile of un-read trade magazines and journals was in danger of tottering over from the small coffee table.

Quinn however did feel productive that Monday morning. Both short and lengthy e-mails were being dispatched with considerable regularity to both peers and subordinates. Quinn regularly checked the inbox anxiously looking for immediate replies from everybody. The tension of waiting somehow seemed exciting to Quinn and inspired Quinn to look for more ways to rapidly communicate. Shortly after 10:15 AM Quinn had dispatched and responded to in excess of fifty e-mails, and left fifteen voicemails for various people.

This is turning into a good day thought Quinn, being highly productive and energetic. Quinn's self-congratulatory moment was about to end!

2. "I'M REALLY NOT IN CONTROL HERE"

The telephone on Quinn's desk rang and Quinn noted on the caller ID display that it was the vice president Andrew's executive assistant Elizabeth Johnston calling. "Good morning Liz", said Quinn in an upbeat voice.

"Andrew has asked me to remind you that you were due at the senior management meeting at 10 AM", replied Elizabeth, in a firm voice and with no acknowledgement of Quinn's cheerful greeting.

Quinn's immediate response was to almost slam the left click function on the mouse to look at the daily schedule on the desktop, whilst inwardly cursing that in the excitement of starting the day with volumes of e-mails Quinn had in fact forgotten to check the day's schedule. There, in full view, was a calendar entry '10 AM to 11 AM Senior Management Meeting'.

Quinn's hands began an uncontrollable shaking, "I'm so sorry Liz, I'll be there in a few minutes."

Grabbing a blank legal pad and a pen, and knowing that a search for the senior management meeting file would take too much time, Quinn left the office and jogged along the corridor to the fire exit and ran up the steps to the floor above. A brisk walk along the corridor to conference room number one took less than thirty seconds. Quinn knocked on the closed-door of the main conference room and entered, closing the door quietly behind.

The large conference room was configured this morning to hold one long table. Along the left-hand side sat the four vice presidents, including Quinn's own vice president Andrew. The remainder of the table was occupied by Quinn's peers - the three other divisional managers (Sally, Joe and Andrea), and three staff from the finance, HR and production departments. The only empty seat was at the far end of the conference table and Quinn self-consciously made a brisk walk towards it.

"I'm sorry I'm late," said Quinn to the assembled group.

It was all that really could be said under the circumstances. The vice president of finance, Helen Goldstaff, as the chair of the meeting, nodded at Quinn, and looked down at her agenda in front of her.

"James," Helen said, addressing the vice president of HR, "could you please give us an update on where we stand with recruiting?"

The meeting then continued for another 15 minutes with updates both from the HR department and the production department. It was then the turn of the finance department to provide the latest financial performance numbers.

"The high-level numbers show us trading above our expected budget," began Helen, "in particular the online training revenue line is 7% higher than we predicted we'd be at this stage in the second quarter." Helen nodded approvingly towards the vice president of production, Julia, who briefly returned the acknowledgement.

"Although overall sales revenue is up," continued Helen, "we are beginning to notice a trend of declining revenue in one of the geographical areas."

Before Helen could continue her point Andrew, the vice president of sales, looked up sharply towards Helen and interjected, "Which area would that be?" Quinn sensed a tension building in the air, as it was clear that Andrew was less than impressed at an attempt to blindside him by a colleague in a meeting in which his direct reports were sitting facing him.

"It's geographical area 'A'," replied

Helen. "As in our areas B, C and D area, A is dominated by the performance of twenty of the on average one hundred customers we have. It's the usual Pareto principle that 80% of the revenue in that division Andrew comes from 20% of your clients."

"Of which I am well aware," replied Andrew even more tersely than before.

"Well," said Helen surveying the group around her, "I understand two of those top 20 clients, who in turn produce a significant proportion of the revenue of the top 20, have become increasingly frustrated with the customer service support they're receiving and as a consequence are ordering less training."

Andrew looked along the table at Quinn and asked if Quinn, as the divisional manager of geographical area A, would like to make a comment. Quinn was temporarily lost for words. In what seemed like an eternity Quinn processed this news. Firstly Quinn knew nothing about it! Secondly, how, Quinn thought, could two of the major clients of the division be dissatisfied with the customer service and dropping their sales orders and yet Quinn knew nothing about it?

Only thirty minutes ago Quinn had been in the office feeling productive and in control, and now the day had descended into an out-of-control chaotic crisis!

Struggling for something to say Quinn looked at Andrew and said the first thing that came into Quinn's mind, "I think I may have dropped the ball on this one Andrew." Andrew stared directly into Quinn's eyes and icily replied, "Well pick it back up again then."

Quinn was conscious that most of the people sitting around the table were now staring awkwardly down at their writing pads. An unnerving silence had settled across the room.

Andrew, as always the calm one, turned back to Helen and said, "I'm aware of the situation and will get an update from Quinn outside of this meeting. It will be circulated to you all by the end of today." It was a firm 'put down' of the issue, and Quinn was impressed.

Helen, sensing that she had lost the initiative, went on to cover two more areas of general interest before announcing, shortly before 10:45 AM that the meeting was over. The assembled group left the conference room fairly quickly. Quinn and Andrew were the only two left in the room. Andrew looked up at Quinn and said firmly, "Go back to your division, get on top of this, and come and see me as soon as you have the full facts." At this he stood up, gathered his few papers and tablet computer, and walked out of the conference room.

Quinn, fighting back the anger that was growing inside towards the team for not briefing her properly, walked very quickly from the conference room along the corridor to the fire exit stairs to get back to the office as fast as possible.

Quinn immediately called the sales manager, Mark Scott, and his two assistants Kate and Jeff, and they arrived within 5 minutes of Quinn getting back from the meeting. In a heated exchange lasting several minutes Quinn demanded to know how this morning's incident had happened and how Quinn had been allowed to be completely blindsided at the meeting.

Mark Scott, an aggressive salesman within an ego of substantial size, defended his position aggressively. He said that he had brought the necessary issues to Quinn's attention over the past week by including highlighted updates in his sales reports. Mark was very self-confident in his posturing, and self-doubt was now slowly creeping in to Quinn's mind. Was it possible that Mark was right and Quinn had, in the busyness of getting things done, missed, or skimmed over, an important briefing document?

Quinn felt the immediate situation was getting out of control – there was too much tension and anger in the office for this to be remotely productive. This was an unnecessarily hastily convened meeting, and Quinn had, again, not prepared for it. Moreover, Quinn's growing sense of self doubt that Mark might actually be correct meant Quinn needed to check the appropriate files quickly.

"Okay guys," said Quinn, "we're not going to achieve anything like this, so get back to work and let me think about this."

Mark, Kate and Jeff left the office and Quinn shut the door behind them. Quinn returned to the desk and wearingly sat down. Where was this day going? This morning seemed so positive, Quinn's energy level had been high, and the flood of productive e-mails and telephone calls that started the day now seemed to be a distant memory.

Quinn sat down in front of the desktop monitor and looked at the email inbox. There were hundreds of unfiled emails to look through. Quinn typed in a search query to begin a look through recent e-mails from Mark to see if he was correct the data had come through in his report. Some 15 minutes later, Quinn had found the information. Mark was correct. However, because Mark did not see the declining customer service and drop in sales as significant he had buried the comment within a report that covered broader areas of performance.

Damn, thought Quinn, I'm really not in control here, and this is verging on a crisis for me.

Quinn composed a short e-mail to Mark, requesting a written response from him, by e-mail by 2 PM that day. Quinn asked for a succinct situation report concerning the two clients, including comment on the customer service issues, past sales, current sales and projected sales. Quinn asked for a recommendation from Mark on the next steps that should be taken with these clients.

This would give Quinn sufficient information to analyze the situation, so Quinn could then go and see Andrew to give him the information he needed.

The e-mail response from Mark arrived on time. Quinn's analysis of the data within Mark's reply showed this was, as Mark had suggested, not a serious situation. The customer service issues appeared to be both minor and isolated and the drop in sales linked to just one product. Moreover, Mark's forward analysis showed that sales in other areas, based on preliminary visits by his sales team to the clients, were about to increase by 15%!

Armed with this encouraging news Quinn contacted Andrew's executive assistant and asked if it would be possible to make an appointment to see him that afternoon to follow-up the morning's meeting. Elizabeth made an appointment for Quinn at 3:30 PM. Determined not to be unprepared for this meeting, Quinn spent the next three quarters of an hour making sure that all the answers Andrew was likely to be seeking on these clients and sales and projections were ready to be presented.

3. AN UNCOMFORTABLE
MEETING WITH ANDREW

Quinn reported to Andrew's outer-office just before 3:30 PM. Although Andrew's office door was open, Elizabeth did not invite Quinn to go in unto exactly 3:30 PM. Andrew was waiting at the small conference table in the corner of his office.

"I've been looking into the customer service and sales issues that were raised in this morning's meeting," began Quinn as they faced each other across the table. "I have some answers here for you which, in my view, show that the issue was not quite as serious as we maybe thought at first."

Then there was an unsettling silence in the room as Andrew stared across the table at Quinn.

"I didn't think there would be a problem," replied Andrew after a while.

"We both see the same data, and I've known these clients for years, so I was expecting you to tell me that Mark was on top of things and there was no real cause for concern." Quinn was now confused, if Andrew knew that why did he not say so this morning?

Before Quinn could say anything Andrew continued "What's of greater concern to me is the morning's meeting, and your performance there."

"Are you not going to talk to me about that?" asked Andrew. Quinn felt uncomfortable. "Well, I'm sorry that I was late but I was buried in a round of backwards and forwards e-mails and took my eye off the clock." Quinn regretted saying that almost as soon as it came out. Andrew was no fool.

"Really?" replied Andrew, "The fact you came into the meeting at all was down to Elizabeth contacting you, and you came with no files or notes. I'll put it out there you'd forgotten about that meeting. Am I right?"

Quinn noticed that Andrew was smiling, in that paternal way he sometimes adopted. Quinn was backed into a corner, but in Andrew there was somebody that could help. "You're right," conceded Quinn "sorry, I had forgotten the meeting. My laptop wouldn't work first thing this morning so I couldn't access my schedule to see what the day looked like, and then I forgot to check my schedule when I arrived in the office as I had so many things on my mind to get down and e-mails and telephone calls to manage, I just got swept up in the momentum of the morning."

Andrew was sitting calmly and reflectively. Quinn thought I've worked for Andrew now for over a month and despite some challenging situations I have seen him in, I've never seen him lose his temper. His level of self-control is admirable.

"How do you control all of your projects?" asked Andrew suddenly.

"Well, I have files on each of my major projects, and keep those close to hand on the desk. I put reminders in my schedule when things are supposed to happen, and my guys know to come to me outside of our regular weekly meetings if there are any key issues that need immediate action. It's at those weekly meetings that I get updates from them on all the issues that are going on. They also know they can e-mail me at any time and keep me posted."

Andrew smiled, "And how is that working out for you?" he said somewhat sarcastically.

Quinn couldn't help but smile in response, "Clearly not very well!"

"I'm pleased," replied Andrew, "with the progress you've made in delegation to your team (*NB: the model is in the first book in this series "It's Your Responsibility Now!"*). The model you came up with is well respected amongst your team and I know they enjoy working with it." Quinn relaxed a little.

"Delegating is one thing," continued Andrew, "but control is something really different. Have you heard of Robert E. Lee?" "Yes", replied Quinn, "Wasn't he one of the American Civil War's greatest generals?"

"That's right. Whilst there are a number of quotes attributed to Lee, the one that comes to mind now is *"I cannot trust a man to control others who cannot control himself."*

Quinn felt embarrassed at the inference that Andrew was making and didn't know what to say.

Andrew continued, "Quinn, your office environment is a disaster. I don't know how you manage to work with so much clutter around you. You must waste hours every day just looking for things you need to refer to. If your office looks like that I can only imagine what your filing system within your e-mails and your desktop folders looks like."

"I don't doubt for one minute you feel

you're on top of things, and I love the energy and excitement that you bring to the workplace," reassured Andrew, "however, when you fail to turn up for senior management meetings, and when you do turn up you're unprepared and unable to answer questions about your division's performance, then I have to question whether you are truly in control and whether your systems are actually working."

Quinn knew deep within that Andrew was right. Every day was flying by in a whirl of frantic activity and Quinn felt energetically keeping many balls in the air at one time was not sustainable in the long run.

"It's difficult Andrew when you're new to the organization to impose your own thoughts and ideas on your division. The division seemed to be running pretty well when I arrived, so it seemed wrong somehow to want to change too much. However, I'm beginning to see now the status quo is not good enough and the sheer pace around here means that I've got to find a way to get this division to run the way that I want it to run - so that I can control it properly and in my own way."

"Exactly," replied Andrew with a sigh, "many people talk about the first one hundred days in a new job and how important those are, and they really are, because once those days have passed you can never recover the newness that you bring to an organization and the opportunity you have to stamp your own personality upon it."

Quinn deeply respected Andrew as a teacher and mentor and felt very comfortable asking him for advice. Quinn knew this was the way the Andrew liked to operate. "I know I need to sort this out myself," said Quinn to Andrew, "but are there any key areas or ideas you think I should focus on initially?"

Quinn had become aware over the four weeks or so that she and Andrew had been working together Andrew liked to deal in outcomes. Andrew rose to the occasion. "Quinn, regardless of our leadership positions we all face three situations each day that we have to manage. Firstly we need to find time to clear up all of the 'stuff' that comes our way. - Emails, voice mails, mail, thoughts and ideas, journals and reports that we need to read etc. Secondly, we have projects that are ours and ours alone we need to work on. Lastly we need to control, lead and inspire our team. We need to find time to do these three things each and every day."

"Those are the three that I would initially focus on managing. In doing so I would suggest you look for a way to consistently structure your day, not in a rigid and inflexible way, but in a way you can adapt and adopt to the circumstances around you. I would also look for ways to both clear the clutter you have around you and find a way of stopping it ever happening again. Most importantly you need to identify what your goals are, both your divisions and your own personal goals – they should act as your overall directional guide as to where your priority focus should be."

Quinn was about to thank Andrew when

he added, "And please don't hesitate to come back and ask me about any of these issues or float some ideas past me. As I've said many times before I'm here to help, and you're an integral part of this team."

At that Andrew stood up, his usual sign a meeting was over, thanked Quinn for coming, and moved towards his desk. As Andrew reached his desk he said, "Quinn, as a senior manager you are paid to *think* as well as *do*. You would do well to remember that." Quinn left the office and headed back down to the second floor.

It was 4 PM when Quinn sat back down behind the desk. On entering the office Quinn had shut the door. Andrew was right, there was no excuse for all of this clutter around the office after four weeks of occupancy. Quinn acknowledged sleep had been difficult for several weeks with so many ideas constantly circulating in Quinn's mind. There were far too many loose ends around here, and of course all this clutter. It was time to tidy up, both physically and mentally!

PART TWO
THE BIG DE-CLUTTER
EXERCISE

4. DE-CLUTTERING THE OFFICE

Quinn had no appointments that evening so decided to stay in the office and commit to a major tidy up and de-cluttering operation. Quinn thought there had to be a logical and systematic approach to this tidy up and decided on the initial creation of stacks of 'stuff'. The first stack would be any item in the office requiring an action of some sort. The second stack would be items to read and review, such as journals and reports. The third stack would be items needing filing or keeping for further reference. Finally there would be the stack of items to be thrown away.

Quinn began at the desk. As the tidy up began and Quinn handled and processed various papers and documents Quinn's mind kept generating ideas and thoughts, either sparked by something that Quinn touched and saw or through some strange recall system which seemed to kick in once the de-cluttering began. Quinn took a pile of blank sheets of paper from the printer machine and placed them centrally on the desk. Each thought that came into Quinn's head was recorded individually on a sheet and then the sheet placed either in the action stack or the reference stack.

After a while Quinn decided there were two more stacks needed! The fifth one was called 'thoughts', and was a place where some ideas that occurred to Quinn, but were not pressing ones, still needed capturing. The sixth stack contained items where a task had been delegated by Quinn and was waiting for the outcome or response – this became known as the 'on-hold' stack.

Once the desktop was clear Quinn moved over to the small worktable in the corner of the office and applied the same process to the papers there. Quinn then emptied the various cardboard boxes of personal items that had been stacked up since Quinn's arrival one month ago. After two hours of activity Quinn began emptying the desk drawers. Here Quinn decided to be completely ruthless - for example how many pens does one person actually need in the desk? Quinn developed a very small stationery supply in the top drawer of pens, notebooks, highlighter pens, a stapler, paper clips and sticky notes. Everything else was thrown away. The remaining desk drawers were emptied completely.

Next Quinn turned on the desktop computer and opened the e-mail account. I really should apply the same process here thought Quinn, and so created new folders within the e-mail account called 'Action', 'Read/Review', 'On-hold', and 'Thoughts'. Quinn's inbox contained literally hundreds of e-mails. Although Quinn was pleased all of these e-mails had been opened and read in some shape or form it was still frustrating they had been left languishing in the inbox. Quinn's commitment was to get the inbox of the e-mail account to zero. One by one Quinn went through the e-mails and moved them into the appropriate folders. Quinn was surprised at how many of these e-mails simply required deleting or filing. After nearly an hour the e-mail account was successfully down to zero.

Quinn's desk was an L-shaped construction. Quinn used the major portion as a writing/working area where it contained the telephone, the desktop monitor and keyboard. On the smaller extension to the L-shape Quinn now placed some plastic trays containing the various stacks that had been created during the de-cluttering exercise. On each tray Quinn placed a handwritten label identifying the contents. Quinn placed one last tray closest to the main desktop and labeled it 'In'.

Quinn sat back and surveyed the now neat and tidy office. Although looking at the trays of work on the side table there appeared to be much more work to do to clear them, Quinn felt a high degree of satisfaction from the tidiness and order now evident in the working space of the office. It was 8:30 PM and Quinn spent the last 15 minutes mounting on the office walls the various personal pictures and certificates which had been in the cardboard boxes, completing the much needed and overdue personal decoration of the office. The office was now very much to Quinn's taste and style. Quinn stood up, stretched and yawned, and walked out of the office to go home to a well-deserved night's rest!

5. THE FIVE-MINUTE RULE

Quinn spent the next morning in the office simultaneously handling the e-mail and telephone traffic whilst tackling the action stack from the night before. Quinn discovered some simple rules could be applied to each and every item in this action stack.

The first was the 'five-minute' rule - if the item could be dealt with in less than five minutes, Quinn would deal with it there and then.

Secondly, by keeping e-mails to less than five sentences in length, or leaving a voicemail with a callback number and a preferred time, Quinn was impressed at how fast items could be dealt with.

Thirdly, those items requiring more than five minutes work were put to one side until the afternoon.

Fourthly, there were a great many items that simply needed delegating.

And finally, despite the filter from last night, Quinn still found items which, once read, simply needed deleting or destroying. Quinn made a note of these processing 'rules' and actions for use later on.

After lunch, and two quick visits from members of the team with issues needing quick decisions, Quinn turned attention to the creation of a filing system. Although determined to live as much as possible in a paperless environment Quinn was realistic enough to realize paper will never disappear completely. However, that was no excuse for creating a complex filing system. Quinn recalled once working for a highly organized lady in a small business. This lady had a remarkable filing system and Quinn decided to adopt the model to use now. The simplicity of the lady's model was in the use of the alphabet.

All paper documents would be contained within simple A4 size plain manila cardboard files. Each file would have a name that best described the contents. These files would then be filed alphabetically. There was no need to use either a numbered system, colour-coded files or sections that were further sub-divided etc.

How now to store my electronic files and documents thought Quinn? Quinn had decided last night one of the changes needed would be to ensure as much of the day-to-day activities Quinn was involved in should be synchronized across all the various technology platforms being used (cell phone, tablet, laptop, desktop etc.) In addition to making it easier to store and find items, synchronization meant a major time-saving in not having to repeat actions. Quinn decided to replicate the alphabetical paper filing system for the electronic files and folders. Surely it made sense to have the two match and be synchronized?

Quinn left the office and went along to the main office supply room and collected a large pile of plain manila folders – Quinn also spotted a label maker in the corner of the room and borrowed that as well. Armed with these two simple tools Quinn quickly created a labeled, alphabetical, filing system and, in less than an hour, cleared all the filing collected from the previous de-cluttering session. Quinn's filing cabinet sat underneath the extension to the side of the desk and contained three drawers. Quinn decided to dispense with hanging folders. This was a simple personal preference, partly caused by the desire to avoid making additional labels for each of the suspending files but also the propensity of these hanging files to eventually bend and collapse as they became overburdened. Moreover, in the past Quinn had found that they tended to take up too much space. Quinn simply placed the files in the drawers and let them support each other.

Quinn decided it would be quicker and more efficient to start the new electronic alphabetical system from scratch, moving all new items in to it today onwards. Then, during quieter periods, Quinn could return to the older items and migrate them over in batches.

Quinn had managed the telephone and e-mail traffic during the day by every fifteen or twenty minutes walking over to the desktop monitor and checking e-mails and voicemails. Although this interrupted the flow with which she was able to bring to solving the organizational and filing challenges and clearing the action tray it did enable Quinn to keep on top of the seemingly endless stream of email traffic coming in.

Quinn finished the working day feeling that over the last twenty-four hours a significant degree of control of the immediate surroundings had taken place. The backlog had been cleared, and a simple system of 'deal within five minutes' or 'delegate', or 'defer', or 'delete', or 'file', was enabling Quinn to keep on top of the current workflow.

6. PROJECT MANAGEMENT

Feeling less overwhelmed Quinn reflected overnight the much bigger issue now needed to be confronted - that of control of projects and control of the division.

On Wednesday morning, after working through more e-mails and dealing with a few staffing issues, Quinn strolled along the corridor to see if any of the three divisional manager colleagues (Sally, Joe and Andrea,) were free for a discussion about control. Quinn found Sally, the divisional manager of geographical area B, sitting at her office desk making a telephone call. Sally gestured to Quinn it was okay to come in and wait. Quinn sat down at Sally's small conference table.

Quinn observed Sally's office was remarkably tidy and well organized. There was a large whiteboard on the wall containing a series of diagrams and lists and well-organized bookshelves. Sally's L-shaped desk, the same as Quinn's, was clutter free. This all looks remarkably similar to Andrew's office, reflected Quinn.

Sally ended the telephone conversation and joined Quinn at the small conference table, "What can I do for you?" asked Sally in a pleasant, engaging manner.

"If you've got a couple of minutes I wonder if I could talk to you about the control model you use for your division?" replied Quinn. Sally hesitated. Quinn continued, "It's just that after the embarrassment of Monday morning (Sally nodded at the recollection of the senior management meeting at which she had also been present) I've been working this week on finally clearing up the clutter and getting settled in and establishing some systems.

Andrew of course has given me a few pointers and said what I need more than anything else is a control model to oversee my division. I know he's right, but rather than reinvent the wheel I wondered if you or Joe or Andrea are currently using something that I could piggyback onto?"

"Oh", smiled Sally, "now I understand." Sally went over to her desk and picked up her tablet computer and returned to the conference table. She opened an application called Asana.com. Sally turned the laptop around so Quinn could see what was on the screen.

Quinn was looking at a dashboard of some kind, which had various forms of data grouped into 'milestones', 'to-dos', and 'project lists'. Sally explained to Quinn how the project management system operated. The same as Quinn, Sally had been fairly overwhelmed during her first few months in the job when she joined the firm last year. In her previous job she had been using a company-wide project management software, which she understood was paid for by the organization on a user basis. Stratum did not operate a culture where centralized systems were used. The CEO was very wary of using one overly dependent system, which could 'crash' and cause the whole organization to grind to a halt.

Sally explained once she had settled into her role she began searching for a customizable system that was either free, or at a sufficiently low cost that she could subsume within her budget. The system she was now using was free for all users, with fees only 'kicking-in' once any stored data, such as files, exceeded a certain storage capacity.

On a pad of paper so Quinn could see Sally sketched out a diagram showing how the project management system was set up and she controlled it and, as a result, her division.

Quinn noted the system was basically simplistic, containing:

1. A 'Project' with a given name for each and every project under Sally's control.

2. A completion deadline (if needed) for the project.

3. A central list showing all the projects being followed.

4. A discussion area for exchange of thoughts, ideas and updates for each project.

5. An area for the sharing of files.

6. Milestone dates when the component parts of each project should be complete.

7. To-do lists of all the action needed to complete each project.

8. Details of the team members responsible for each To-do or milestone.

"If it's one of my personal projects I set it up myself, establishing milestone dates, to-dos and linking appropriate files. If it's a project one of my team will be working on I ensure that one of them sets up the initial information in the system. It rarely takes more than fifteen minutes to input the milestones, the to-dos, set access permissions and attach files, if all the necessary planning has already taken place for the project."

Quinn was extremely impressed with the system's simplicity and user access and was already beginning to see a number of uses and adaptations of this model for the division.

Sally continued, "One of the strengths of the program is I can also allow our clients to have access to the website to see the projects we are managing for them. Then we have full transparency with them on how we're doing, and through the 'discussion' function they can even take part in a Q&A style continuous debate and ask questions directly of us."

Quinn was taking plenty of notes on the notepad and asked, "It looks great Sally, but how do you know the information in any single project is up-to-date? Surely if one of the staff were trying to hide they were behind on a project, or in trouble, they could simply input the information they wanted you to read, and hide the truth?"

"It's about accountability and responsibility," replied Sally, "when I introduced system I amended all of the staff job descriptions to include a section of full compliance with this project management system. We ran group-training sessions to make sure everybody knew how it would operate, and it also enabled me to get full buy-in from everyone. I also include compliance with the system as part of the annual staff performance review. It's also very rare that somebody is running one of these projects completely on their own, so there is always a element of a safety check involved from the second or third team member."

Sally thought carefully for a moment and then added, "Of course, just because you have a system running it doesn't mean you personally can abdicate your leadership for the results. It still means I have to use my judgment when I analyze the data I'm receiving through it, look for trends, and question and probe and satisfy myself the data is valid. But I see such work as part of my role as the divisional manager anyway, regardless of whether there was a model like this in place or not."

"I now see what Andrew was getting at when he said to me that one of the three things I need to do every day is make sure I have the time in the day to control and lead my teams – which in reality means time to think." added Quinn.

"And I bet he said the other two were clearing the stuff that comes across our desk every day and dealing with your own personal projects?" joked Sally with a smile on her face. They both laughed knowing that she was right. Quinn felt greatly encouraged Sally had clearly been through the same challenging settling-in period as Quinn, and Andrew had established some flexible enough boundaries for Sally to solve the problem herself. He was now simply doing the same for Quinn.

Sally took Quinn through a number of different scenarios she had encountered over the months in the project management system, including the manner in which she had created dashboard reports. She then showed Quinn how the discussion function worked by calling two of her team online to quickly discuss an issue she had been talking through on the telephone with a client when Quinn had first entered. Finally Sally passed on the website address to Quinn for the sign-up and suggested that once Quinn was settled and comfortable with the program they meet again when Sally could answer any early questions Quinn may have.

Quinn walked back along the corridor to the office thinking hopefully another piece of the puzzle had just fallen into place.

Over the next few days Quinn set up the project management model and initially imported personal projects to make sure that Quinn was comfortable with the way the model operated. Quinn then turned attention across the division with its sales, marketing, and training delivery functions and went to each of the four managers and told them to ensure all of the projects were up-to-date by the beginning of the following week. At which time, Quinn informed them, there would be a meeting where the new project management model would be unveiled, plans for training to take place, eventually leading to all the division's projects being loaded into the system. Quinn informed the four managers they would then be responsible for training their direct reports in the use of and compliance with the new system. They would be fully operational within one week.

7. A STRUCTURE FOR THE TYPICAL DAY

Over the weekend Quinn focused on two tasks. Firstly, inspired by the de-cluttering and new organization in the office, Quinn decided to undertake an identical project at home – calling it another form of synchronization! Nothing was spared from the de-cluttering whirlwind, which engulfed the house that weekend as Quinn went through cupboards, drawers, wardrobes, the garage and sought to create order and systems all around!

It was on the Sunday evening Quinn began to consider the second task - there was still one element missing from the office organizing project. It was some form of bridge, Quinn felt, which needed to be in place between the project management control model and the reality of endlessly demanding day-to-day activities. Quinn decided to list all of the challenges and frustrations that occurred during the course of a typical working week:

1. E-mail traffic was constant and there was always an expectation of instantaneous reply.

2. Voicemail tag, a form of game where somebody leaves you a message, you reply to this message and you leave them a message and then they reply and leave you a message and so on and so on - a daily frustration.

3. The telephone did seem to ring quite a lot and Quinn was never sure whether to interrupt the focus of the moment and answer the 'phone or leave it.

4. There were many websites that Quinn needed to visit to obtain updates and

news during the course of the day.

5. Quinn liked an 'open door' policy and wanted to be accessible to the staff. However, an open door policy means there was never an exclusive time to singularly focus on projects without being interrupted.

6. Hardcopy 'real' mail needed integrating into the virtual mailbag coming in through e-mail.

7. Quinn would often have thoughts and ideas about the division and, like all human beings, have no way of controlling when those thoughts and ideas would visualize. There had to be a way of capturing these in a way they could be retrieved at a later stage.

8. With a smart 'phone, tablet computer, and laptop there needed to be an overall system in place that could be synchronized and accessible 24 hours a day if required.

Finally, Quinn believed the system needed had to be simple and minimalistic. Quinn knew from past experience if systems become too cumbersome, or too complicated, they wouldn't be used and the benefits would be lost. It seemed the missing piece now to make life function effectively was some form of structure to a typical day – a core system to rely on and underpin the various activities. Quinn was not naive enough to believe that every day would be a perfect orderly day but also realized at the same time it should be possible to create a framework that was flexible enough to cope with the rigors and demands of most days Quinn might face.

Having the discipline to set up a daily routine, and to stay with it, would be difficult and require significant focus. Quinn thought of Andrew and his incredible ability to always be prepared and the focus he brought to each and every occasion. Quinn considered him to be the most 'in the moment' person Quinn had ever met. How did he do it Quinn wondered? It had to be his power to focus thought Quinn, but where does one get that power of focus from? Quinn recalled attending a seminar at a conference many years ago on the subject of focus and recalled the keynote speaker saying the human mind is, despite all the modern talk of multitasking, only truly capable of focusing on one item at a time. The key to powerful focus must therefore be to eliminate distractions and simply do one thing at a time. The keynote speaker had advocated such an approach and was adamant there was plenty of empirical data out there to prove focusing on one thing until its completion was an incredibly powerful function and yielded exceptional results. Quinn had never really been in a position since that seminar to overly worry about needing to put that kind of focus into place, but this situation was different. Now it was real.

In a journal Quinn brainstormed some potential ways to manage a typical day, based on Andrew's three priorities (clear the 'stuff' which comes in every day; control and lead the team; work on personal projects). Six segments emerged from this brainstorm:

•**Project Time:**	•Maximum of 2 hours •Complete the 3 actions
•**Process Time:**	•Handle all email, voicemail, mail, thoughts, ideas, etc. •Do it; Place on hold; Delete it
•**Control Time:**	•Review all projects •What, when, how, by whom •Email, visit, call, question, suggest etc.
•**Discretionary Time:**	•Use time to work on personal projects •Think, plan •Read, review
•**Process Time:**	•Handle all email, voicemail, mail, thoughts, ideas, etc. •Do it; Place on hold; Delete it
•**Review Time:**	•Review 'Action Required' •Select the next day's top 3 action items

Quinn next allocated some approximate timings, giving the segments such structure:

Project Time: 08:30 AM – 10:30 AM

Process Time: 10:30 AM – 11:00 AM

Control Time: 11:00 AM – 1:00 PM

Discretionary Time: 2:00 PM – 4:00 PM

Process Time: 4:00 PM – 4:30 PM

Review Time: 4:30 PM – 5:00 PM

This will take care of the typical day, but Quinn needed a broader review process that would help identify upcoming events (for example Quinn thought how effective it could be to prepare on a Monday for a meeting not taking place until Thursday – actually turning up for the meeting well read and briefed!). Some form of a weekly review was needed thought Quinn – a chance to look out over the coming week and all the projects Quinn and the team were working on. This would be the time and place for reviewing the 'goals' Andrew had spoken about, ensuring the week's activities were focused upon them.

The final element would be a system of automated reminders where trying to remember events and deadlines would no longer have to be at the mercy of Quinn's mind – a simple email or text message would be scheduled to arrive as a reminder. Quinn searched around the web for a free system which could deliver timely reminders both by text message and email – eventually settling on followupthen.com. Quinn signed up and was operational in a few minutes, having set up reminders to be sent in hours, days, weeks, even months in advance!

Quinn had been trying to decide on a single platform to use consistently each and every day to control everything – thinking for example how it could be possible to sit in a meeting and have every piece of information that may be needed instantly at Quinn's fingertips. Of all the electronic and paper aids available Quinn eventually settled on using the tablet computer.

Quinn had been extremely impressed with how Sally had all the project management information accessible through the application on her tablet. Quinn had been integrating the most important spreadsheets, documents, presentations, the calendar, email, onto the tablet both through the organization's 'Cloud' and also the Asana.com project management application. Finally, Quinn signed up for a social media dashboard called Hootsuite.com (Quinn had asked the IT department to send an analysis of all the websites Quinn had visited in the past ten days and found the three most frequently visited were social media, where Quinn kept in touch with industry contacts, new products, emerging trends). Now, one dashboard (also available on the tablet) gave Quinn instant integrated access to all the main sites subscribed to. More time saved!

Finally, with the tablet allowing Quinn to see and access all the important data and documents, Quinn was able to just take the tablet everywhere and be in a constant state of control. Quinn decided to use the tablet to take notes (using the handwriting application penultimate.com saving the need to carry paper – the notes from the meeting could then be instantly emailed as a PDF back to Quinn's inbox.

Also Quinn could take photographs with the tablet directly into the penultimate note, capturing whiteboard brainstorming, documents, etc.). The tablet's voice recorder would be used to capture thoughts and ideas, and the Dragon Dictate voice recognition application to save time by dictating short emails and documents.

PART THREE
BEING IN CONTROL!
8. A NEW DAY

Quinn walked into the office Monday morning at 8:30 AM, turned on the desktop monitor and tablet, no program was now set to default to open - the email inbox would remain closed until Quinn was ready to view it later – no pop ups or alerts about incoming messages either would distract Quinn from the important work to be done each morning. On the list of action items prepared in advance Quinn noted three tasks requiring action that morning. Each of the tasks had been assigned an estimate of time, so Quinn selected the one that would take the longest, knowing it was most likely to be the most difficult one. Clearing the most difficult task first thing in the morning would be a good psychological boost for the remainder of the day. The task took thirty minutes and Quinn ignored three incoming telephone calls during that time, knowing they were going to voicemail.

Quinn continued onto the next two tasks, keeping the office door shut (Quinn's team had been informed that 8:30 AM until 11 AM most mornings was Quinn's 'project time' and Quinn was not to be disturbed), and by 10:30 AM the three most important tasks in Quinn's projects had been completed. That meant three more projects were one step closer towards conclusion and momentum was being maintained across a broad spectrum of activity.

After a short break for some coffee and to collect the morning mail Quinn returned to the office and opened the e-mail management system. Quinn called this the 'process time'. By not knowing what was in the inbox Quinn had not, for the past two hours, been distracted by any pressing issues. If anything had been extremely urgent internally then someone would have come to find Quinn.

There were 30+ e-mails to clear, and applying the 5-minute rule of fast decision-making Quinn was able to clear all of those e-mails in just over half an hour. Although the telephone had rung a total of five times since Quinn had walked in that morning only two of those calls resulted in voice mails and Quinn recorded the content of those and placed them in the plastic in-tray, ready for when Quinn would manage telephone calls later that day. Within the hardcopy mail there was one important trade journal, which, with a cursory glance through, seemed to have some interesting and relevant articles. Quinn left the office and walked along the corridor to Maria Jacobs' office (one of the two Training Section managers). Quinn handed over the journal and asked Maria to circulate it amongst the staff and ask them to read the articles, précis those that were relevant and circulate the précis across the division for others to read. Quinn asked for a copy also to be sent to Quinn's office. Now Quinn did not need to read the entire journal! The power of delegation, smiled Quinn!

The 'project time' and the 'process time' were now complete. Quinn shut down the e-mail system again and entered the 'control period' of the day. Using the project management tool Quinn spent the next two hours reviewing all of the milestones and to-dos for the various projects Quinn's division was working on. Quinn was mentally setting out to obtain answers to the following questions:

1. What should be happening?

2. When should it be happening?

3. Who should be doing it?

Through a series of personal visits, telephone calls, participation in the online discussion groups within the various projects, and the sending of some e-mails (which

Quinn compiled with email in its 'offline' mode – knowing the emails would dispatch when Quinn changed the system to 'online' later that day, and again avoiding being distracted by incoming emails whilst working), Quinn was able in a short period of time to gain a very good sense of how the division was functioning.

Again Quinn had adopted a simple model here. Quinn would review the data presented within the project management system, analyze it, and most importantly, think about it. Finally Quinn would decide whether any action was needed. The action may even be to decide to do nothing as everything was on target.

It was a simple but effective and fast decision-making process. Once the 'control period' was over Quinn moved into 'discretionary time'. This was always the time between completion of the 'control period' and 4 PM in the afternoon. The discretionary time was Quinn's 'thinking time', it was a time for reading, it was a time for returning telephone calls or being available to receive telephone calls. It was only a closed-door period when Quinn needed time to think. It was a time also when Quinn would arrange meetings with staff or simply go on a fact-finding walkabout to visit the team (armed with the all important tablet!).

At 4 PM it was time for the second process period of the day, Quinn repeated what happened at 11 AM in the morning when e-mails and voice mails were cleared.

At 4:30 pm, as the day came to a close, Quinn returned to the project management tool and reviewed the milestones of the various projects and decided what would be the three to five most important tasks that needed completing the next day. The criteria for selecting these tasks was always the same:

1. They had to be important.

2. They had to have long-term or lasting value.

3. They would continue to move Quinn or the division towards major goals and

objectives.

With the following day outlined, tasks set, all in-boxes empty, Quinn tidied the desk, locked the cupboards and drawers and left the office for home – comfortably on time, in control and relaxed! In the end, Quinn reflected, being in control of oneself is the crucial first step. Have a system or process in place you can trust and use it constantly to reinforce it as a positive habit – it becomes second nature, a form of autopilot. In one week, thought Quinn, I have turned a chaotic situation around into one of a calm, controlled and highly efficient operation. What a difference a week can make!

The End

9. SUMMARY OF KEY LEARNING POINTS

To summarize Quinn's organized approach to the day:

Daily Structure:

Each day has a basic framework, structured yet flexible:

Project Time: 08:30 AM – 10:30 AM

Process Time: 10:30 AM – 11:00 AM

Control Time: 11:00 AM – 1:00 PM

Discretionary Time: 2:00 PM – 4:00 PM

Process Time: 4:00 PM – 4:30 PM

Review Time: 4:30 PM – 5:00 PM

Project Time:

1. Start every day by working for up to two hours on major projects, not reading/answering emails. Quinn had informed the team about this system, ensuring they no longer expected instant replies to their emails.

2. Keep the to-do action list to a maximum of three important tasks to complete per day.

Process Time:

3. On two occasions (of less than 30 minutes) during the day Quinn had been able to process all incoming mail and telephone calls.

4. By shutting down email and incoming telephone calls Quinn had eliminated, as much as practically possible, unnecessary distractions enabling Quinn to complete several hours of important focused project work – every day.

5. Quinn has delegated, (and through that process both empowered and engaged the team), a significant element of the routine work that came across the desktop, empowering the team members to become more responsible and accountable.

6. Quinn now operates under the 5 minute decision making rule – constantly asking the question 'can this item be completed in 5 minutes or less, if yes then deal with it immediately.'

Control Time:

7. By using a project management system, and ensuring all the team members actively used it as well, Quinn has achieved a controlling overview of all of the division's activities, taking corrective action as required.

8. Quinn constantly remembers the leader's role is to be 'in the helicopter', hovering above all the action where everything can be seen, and only 'coming down' when intervention is required.

9. By using systems and processes which can be accessed and used on a tablet computer Quinn is able to have instant and continuous access to real time data on the tablet device which can be easily transported with Quinn to visit team members, attend meetings and visiting clients.

Discretionary Time:

10. Quinn has achieved a minimum of one hour per day of discretionary time to read and think.

11. Quinn has been accessible to team members several hours of the day and made personal visits to key team members.

Review Time:

12. Quinn spends the last 15 – 30 minutes of each day planning the next day's important tasks.

13. Quinn plans the week ahead by always scanning, at the end of the week, all the projects, meetings and tasks to see what the

coming priorities will be.

Being in control of the day:

14. Quinn has established the three pillars of daily activity necessary to be able to lead effectively: One - clear the 'stuff' that comes in everyday; Two - work on personal projects; Three - control and the lead the team.

15. Quinn invested time in de-cluttering Quinn's mind, the office (and the home) environment, creating simple alphabetical filing systems, and committing to ensure clutter did not return.

16. Quinn has developed the habit of 'dumping' from the mind random thoughts and ideas into a safe place where they can be retrieved later. Quinn keeps a selection of note pads close to hand, and uses the voice recorder function on the smart phone and tablet.

17. Quinn was leaving the office at a reasonable hour and not taking any work home!

ABOUT THE AUTHOR

Mark Hollingsworth was born and raised in the United Kingdom. After a short career in the banking and insurance sectors he was commissioned into the Royal Air Force, graduating from the Royal Air Force College Cranwell in 1987. Mark saw service in the United Kingdom, Belize, Germany and Canada, serving in a variety of leadership roles in the administration branch. He retired from the Royal Air Force in 2003 in the rank of squadron leader and now lives in Canada.

Since that time Mark has gained extensive leadership experience as a CEO, Executive Director, Vice President and Director in a variety of organizations. In 2006 he published his first book on leadership ('Leadership: The Basics') and has since undertaken numerous lecturing and speaking engagements on the subject of essential leadership skills, helping him become one of the world's thought leaders in the basic skills of leadership.